Allow Only Joy

a selection
of poems by
John Ellison Davies

Acknowledgments:

Poems in this selection have appeared previously in
Ulitarra, Quadrant, Eureka Street, The Australian, The Age,
Adelaide Review, Newcastle Herald, Southerly, Fremantle
Arts Review, Overland, Northern Perspective, Mattoid, the
Canberra Times, Phoenix Review, Fine Line, the Sydney
Morning Herald, and Webber's Magazine.

Individual poems have been broadcast on 2RRR-FM and
ABC Radio National's A First Hearing and Poetica.

Knock Knock was first performed by Mr Dick Hughes at
Woollahra Library, Sydney, on Tuesday 18 February 1992.

CONTENTS

LUNCH

what becomes of them

the red napkin, the soup
her nervous nail polish
tapping the marble table

her insulted mouth
closing on lasagna and salad

the chilled dew of chablis
on her peach coloured lips

her sceptical shoulders
when she speaks

and her skin
shimmering resentment
when he speaks

what becomes of them
when the table is cleared
and she leaves to invent
a life without miracles

WOMAN, CHILD, MAN

another journey begins
the swollen breast blue-veined
hungrily seeks the hungry mouth
and the child is beautiful
of course, impossible to believe
that what we have made
is not beautiful

the young couple are different
people now, they can fold
the world in a basket
in the child's cry
they hear an older voice
telling them how different they are

each surprised childish
breath reminds them
tyres glide, the road
tightens home, curious
new eyes mirror
a neon-lit kiss

in ecstasy
we breed our own judges

HONEY

tell me the story
again, please
while we have time

explain

the waiting

this poison

these useless wings

and why we dream
of a dizzy
perfumed ceremony
we have never seen

MOUNTAIN POEM

we question the morning
where to begin and morning's
crazy face questions us

with a light grin
through cracked
wooden shutters, a sceptical
pattern on the wall
we tease with shadows

shall we
answer first

shall we
introduce ourselves
to the clouds

the early clouds that graze
at our door and sulk
for lost moonlit pasture?

2 a.m.

silence thickens, wine
still hums in the blood
and coffee is a scalding
blessing, muddy, intense
as a new thought forming

is all forgiven?

it seems possible
at this empty musical hour
when words mean more
and carry further

when whipped by promises
we tend to the horizontal
mouths open for passion
ears made for confession

and our whispers linger
like thin wild notes
on a violin upstairs
never quite forgotten

THE EMBRACE

"you have to love them"
I tell her "It's your only
defence"

she is puzzled
at first, then memory
blooms as it will
when a storm has passed

recognition rainbows
in her hazel eyes
there is a clue
of eagerness on the map

her indelicate history
delicately etched
sweats like glass
in the palm she offers

pressing
gently enough
to shatter worlds

MUST IT BE SO?

it must be so

as the gathering storm
impartial

holds its breath

each raindrop mirrors
earth, ocean, mountains

trembles
lovingly

and begins
its fall

this is the law

there are
no exceptions

allow only joy

REVELATION

this rain falls
on our dry spectacle
like a soft accusation
sweeping the city grey

in this rain
illusions rust through
false obligations tarnish
unrealistic hopes lie sodden
irrelevant as a newspaper
pulped in the sighing gutter

this rain teaches:
enough heaviness, truth
does not weigh so much

what matters?
two small tattoos
on my lover's breasts
and the taste
of her drowsy beauty

A QUESTION

I have heard you

swayed in the lilt
of your voice
like an anemone
filtering its life
from the tilt
of afternoon tides

tossed
from side to side
from sense to sense
of all our possibilities

do I know you?

yes or no
either answer might be
a betrayal
a drowning

UPSTAIRS

an awkward drawer
jammed, pushed
scrapes like thunder

a bump
and sudden silence
could mean murder

a woman speaks
her intention obscure
through plaster and floor
she whistles, I speculate
on the shape of her mouth

life is so interesting
when you don't know
your neighbours

CRITICAL MASS

slack morning limps in
our narrow street, a faint
hope bellows from the squat
brick church, people sit
a medley of coughs and bumps

the priest hesitates
(there is already
one loud letter
on the Bishop's quiet desk)
but refreshed by an early
baptism his tide rises

he is joined to the rock
and his wrecked children
as sea is married to sky
his bliss is a holocaust, frantic
as a hungry gull's cry

he preaches:
forgive us Lord
for we know exactly
what we are doing

at the back of the church
a pen allergic to paradox
is scratching

PAPER CUTS

tick tock
ticky tock

seconds pound
thin skin
hours weigh
blood's heavy
gravity, I cling
to a page
with a pen
and paper cuts

what time is it
in Soweto?
what time is it
in Prague?

ticky tock

gravity is harder
in some places
than others, always

and everywhere
paper cuts

ALLEGORY

he was not a bad man
only a poor painter

big-boned
like our sons
and polite
to our daughters

tough as a goat
or a saint he climbed
our hills in the hot hours
while we slept

and later
when he drank with us
he talked so well
he made our sunsets longer

we thought he understood

but why
did he paint it that way
the great painting
you can see
in the great museum

why did he paint
our fields ablaze

and the lovers' arms
legs, bent, tense
as sunlight between vines?

TREMOR

to one
half asleep
it seemed the bells
rang first
heavy tongued
as his own
stuttering prayers

but then
the statue moved
and he knew
statues do not move
not even holy ones

and he knew
there would be a death

ADVICE

if you would shepherd her
where the world holds hands
read in her touch
a finger-tip code

ask what can you be
that only you can be to her
what can you say
that only you can say to her

remember, no king
makes a wave indecisive
no watchmaker bullies an hour
no wave or hour delays
desire's grained time-table

DICK HUGHES AT THE SHAKESPEARE HOTEL

the magician enters
through engraved doors you see
and doors you cannot see, larger
than the sum of his disguises
chevalier, citizen, chief
engineer of the last train,
master of memory and curiosity,
piano man

his left hand
knows what his right
hand is doing

striking, under a blue moon,
keys to selves we see and selves
we cannot see, girls
who don't lie (not much),
mean firemen, wining boys,
beer-drinking women

improvising certainties

FLOWERS, PERFUME, GLASNOST

unsure
which way to hop

I hop

and collide
with you

again

let's step outside
history

take a laughing
step sideways, turn

and play
a more interesting

game

THESE THINGS SHE KNOWS

"even friendship is a way
of passing the time..."

she knows

her cappuccino, stirred, suggests
dimensions of self-pity
too precise for tears

she knows
how small she is
how great her needs

knowing, she rages
calm as a gambler
losing everything, spun
on the last turn
of the wheel, knowing
it is the end

calm as an angel
who made a mistake
shut out forever
from the elite of love

MOONLIGHT SONATA

wake up
last night there was something
I wanted to tell you
but you were diving
too far down in dreams
when I shook you
your body a limp marker
showing where you had been
and where you would return
telling me not to follow

incomplete, I tried to write

to discover
among the broken words
in my clumsy quarry
a likeness of your dream
a submerged language
you might answer

at five
a black moth fluttered
under the lamp, its desperate wings
stained my pages

wake up
there is something
I want to ask you

HYENA

we lost our nerve
over the fettuccine, our vegetables
are limp, the casserole dry
our jaws ache

no need to explain

in our polite kitchen
gourmet Time itself lies
raw, marinating

no need to explain
today's expressionless frenzy
or tomorrow's salmon-pink lure

DUET 1

there is no escaping
this disgrace, we are

a passenger's numb
dream in a train
on another track

we are the light at sea
and the points of doubt
within the light
the silhouettes on deck

walking, waking
into a future
we did not make

DUET 2

the last page
of the last chapter
of honesty's rule book
says smash the gate's
shy lock, dance
through fear's nettles
into the final garden

if we weep there -
most people are
at their best in tears –

we can be
a surprised face
at each other's window
forever tapping
surprising ourselves

TRISTESSE

in his imagination
the women he has loved
meet for coffee, somewhere inexpensive

they have not read
the same books, not enjoyed
the same paintings, music, films

they are tall, small,
bold, evasive, slender,
rounded, dark, fair, unalike
in style and colour of dress,
shoes, handbags, eyes

and yet together
they are as harmonious
as coral, and not once
do they talk about him

POOR JILL

"I did it again
didn't I?" she asks

her loyal pot-plants
offer trembling buds, mute fruit
from sympathetic stems

she finishes
last night's whisky
neat, as if the answer
could be round
as the taste of whisky

round

as the moon
glimpsed over
a lover's shoulder

perhaps he

perhaps she

questions
are such awkward shapes

she dances
to the applause
of symmetrical leaves

15 WISDOM STREET

the woman next door
is not talking to her husband
she rakes a garden argument
punishes leaves, brawls with flowers
frustrated by the strength of weeds
kneels on a stone and swears

inside the house
her husband smokes
and reads the paper, turns
each urgent page amazed
that he is not news

he wonders who writes
true histories of pain, of hate

newsprint stains
his fingers like guilt

THE SPHINX AT YOUR DOOR

at this pebbled frontier
steps a lame man
singing heads I win
tails I win

free of the leaping herd's
nostalgia for the precipice

lost
in the dusty interval
between the bubble sun
and bubble moon
(those liars)

all that is outside
him torrents in him
but he sings

I am a porous man
heads I win
tails I win

MOTHER

she is an oracle
the tenderness

and lust of centuries
scream through her

history's tiny feet
kick with her pulse

at this fierce moment
she is a goddess

initiated
in the pain of creation

already

resenting

the stretchmarks

RESCUE

as the chasm widens
throw over a rope
and hold tight as if
our life depends on it
(our life does) keep
the icy distance
small and bridgeable

what kind of rope?
how do we fasten it?
do we hammer the pins
into our bones?

you see

sooner or later
every metaphor
pierces flesh

KNOCK KNOCK

it is I

the well-mannered poet
in my coat
of many colours
and red shoes

prematurely grey

one-eyed lord
of blind furry words

master of mirrors

the nervous heart's
early warning

eavesdropper

(I know
when you've been
bad or good)

story teller

trickster

trust me

hey!

I'm talking to you

LITTLE OXFORD ST.

old men sleep
in the back
of abandoned cars
warm in muscat
dreams under dirty

overcoats

plastic garbage bags
torn by dogs reveal
tin smiles, ash,
rotted fruit, letters
not worth keeping,

small bones

old men wake like Thomas
who had to touch to believe

EVERYDAY MASTERPIECE

enthroned
on their cool verandah

the old ones

connoisseurs
of light and shade

resolve
all problems
of proportion

each fragile gesture
a brush-stroke
in a self-portrait

nearing completion

SURFACE TENSION

the lead weight

of the ordinary
is necessary fishing
chance's luminous pools

or we are flies
hovering sun-struck
all buzz, blind
to its promising bubbles

deaf to a brute breath
that waits under lilies
and welcomes splashing fools

SUGAR-CUBISM

in her orchestral
affections I hear

the flute
of a lie

embarrassed
hidden
behind dull
earnest drums

busy strings
weave easy doubt
to taut certainty

performance
for a shocked
audience of one

IN THE GARDENS

he sees all

the dull statue
splashed green
adored by the fountain

the young couple
eating chicken, the roaming
delighted licking dog

and the lonely man
with his loaf of bread
pigeons' claws on his wrist
like a woman's fingernails
himself a scavenger poisoned
by tossed crumbs of laughter

seeing all,
a passionate sparrow
crowns himself emperor

NOT WORTH TALKING ABOUT

for two weeks
I have considered
the fall and curl
of your hair as fragrant
comment, a hint
of lost enthusiasm
trying to grow

to me

now you tie
your hair back
in a bun

your eyebrows
are sad caterpillars
aimed at me

this is the beginning
of obsession

and you say

it's not
worth talking about

THE METHOD

why do men
and women argue?

this one writes itself
in a rhythm of satin

words lean
like dominoes, like us
to a conclusion

THE SLOW LEARNERS

the familiar words
blister our lips

not again
yes, again

darling/idiot

continue/yes

this time
we will not
make the mistake

this time
we will prove
need is deaf
our love-making
will keep the cats
awake

THE WINGS OF A COMPROMISE

pluck out
today's negatives
like brown teeth
from a mouth of protest
cut the mole
small, dark, benign
from reluctant hand or leg

give wings
to what remains

it will fly
only a moment to nest
and nurse soft scars

but perhaps
the moment
will be unique

GAMBLER

lose? win?
what have I won? lost?

impossible to tell

my system
is not numerical

it is a system
of moods
mine, or yours

a system of hints
and promises

a system
without limits

GIVE JUDAS A KISS

you accuse me
I accuse you
quickly, as dogs
bark and jump
at any high-
walled excuse

retreat is agreed
as quickly

rough tongues cool
in pride's ample
shade

and why not? Judas
has no quarrel with Judas

A POET'S LIFE

(for Michael Dransfield)

not what you'd call
a life really
more a sequence of encounters
a collection of misunderstandings
which somehow don't add up

with luck the poems add up
singly, together, alive
with the intensity given
to each encounter, glowing
in each misunderstanding

this is how you live
well, it is your choice

if you must fill blank pages
nobody asked you to fill
if you seek
that heat for your kiln
to inject baked beauty
under the skin of a poem
what do you expect
if not a weary addicted art
then a weary addicted artist?

priceless fool
didn't they tell you?
nobody thanks a volunteer

TO THE LEGISLATORS

I, the people,
have waited patiently

I gave you my vote
and you conspired against me,
my friends, family and children

I revoke your power

I, the people, may govern
myself in any way I choose

you are dismissed

you will not be forgiven
but you will not be punished

your lives will be spared

go now

MILLION DOLLAR POEM

from an unknown author
it appeared, quite unexpectedly,
in The New Yorker

short and simple
it flashed sparks
of all known longing
and fear and heartache

it was a wonder
reprinted everywhere,
downloaded, stencilled
on T-shirts
and coffee cups

it still earns
considerable royalties

the author
never wrote another poem

1789 RAP
(respect to Snoop Dogg)

state of it

people don't know who they are
don't know where they're going
or what they want
watching someone cook on TV
watching Kardashians

that's no life
read a book, fool

7 dollars 25 an hour minimum wage
that's not a job
that's slavery with pocket money

1789, 1917
some shit went down
coming again

talking to the one per cent
with your super-yachts
think you can sail away
think again

read a book, fool

I COULD BE A BAD MAN

I could be a bad man
if I let myself go

I could be a politician
make promises
to bigoted stupid people
listen to their pettiness
tell them what they want to hear

once elected
property developers, I will make it
Christmas for you all year round
in the bleak, ripe, rotting suburbs

Big Tobacco - call me -
laws that are made
can be unmade
you know what I'm saying

or I could be a radio personality
and offend everyone
except bigoted stupid people
who would love me

my salary would be astronomical

ladies, form an orderly queue

MISTAKES

I have been counting
the mistakes in my life

I count eight big ones
between 1970 and 1980

but then only four in
the following twenty years

and four minor errors
in the last fifteen

it's encouraging

PERSONALITY

it's still sound
holding up

it will get you
where you're going

it's not fast, reliable I'd say,
a classic, not many
like this around

eh? well, that
patch of rust
has always been there

it's amazing
what you can do
with a hammer

THREESOME

in the beginning
it was a way
of filling gaps
in the conversation

he'd lost interest
in her pottery
she in his poetry

they both
adored Felicity

she wasn't interested
in anything

THINK TWICE

think once, think twice

as often as it takes

don't rush

better to think
once, twice

than to announce
like a duck
who has seen
another pond's future

"it works"

NEARLY THERE

pronouncing his own name
he sounds doubtful

his explanations are one degree
more fluent than a stammer

he always gets it wrong
too casual, too possessive
too weak, too strong
too early, too late

how can I tell him
he's almost got it right?

STREAMING

I walk into the room
where my wife is watching television

"What's this shit?", I ask, casual

"Colin Farrell's in it",
she says, inscrutable

I walk into the room
where my wife is watching television

"What's this shit?", I ask
with a hint of aggression

"Alexander Skarsgård's in it",
she says, serene

My wife walks into the room
where I am watching television

"What's this shit?", she asks

"Chloë Sevigny's in it", I say

she quivers with indecision

DEMOCRACY

my wife tells me
many things

a new plan
a new rule

(a towel must hang
here not there)

and the plans
and rules keep changing

(a towel must hang
there not here)

sometimes
I am not in the same room
when she tells me

but I have been told

if I protest I did not hear
she says "You're going deaf."

if I claim an equal vote
she brings out the big gun:

"You've forgotten
how to be part of a couple."

STAGGERING MAN

immediately I know
I cannot help him

he mimes his grief
stares angrily at the gate
at me and away from me
trying to tell me

he moans
sorrow on the lawn
until anguish clots his throat

the wind raises
around him
a cloak of leaves

how many
endure without love?

www.ingramcontent.com/pod-product-compliance
Lightning Source LLC
Chambersburg PA
CBHW071451150726
48000CB00006B/2520